Social Media Marketing and Blogging for Profit

Turn Your Business or Personal Brand Online Presence into a Money Making Machine with a Responsive Blog - A Copywriting Secrets Guide for Beginners

By

Michael Branding

render any resulting actions solely under their purview. There are no scenarios in which the publisher or the original author of this work can be in any fashion deemed liable for any hardship or damages that may befall them after undertaking information described herein.

Additionally, the information in the following pages is intended only for informational purposes and should thus be thought of as universal. As befitting its nature, it is presented without assurance regarding its prolonged validity or interim quality. Trademarks that are mentioned are done without written consent and can in no way be considered an endorsement from the trademark holder.

Table of Contents

Chapter 1 - Basic Concepts

Social media marketing is a powerful way for businesses, professionals and organizations of all sizes to find and connect with returning or potential customers or users. Social marketers thus create company Facebook pages and accounts on Twitter, Instagram, Pinterest and other major social networks to reach this goal.

However, not all of these professionals really have clear goals and well defined strategies, nor an in-depth knowledge of how social media interact with consumers and how they can use this interaction to increase brand awareness, boost sales and profits, and create brand loyalty. This is why we strongly recommend that you understand how social media marketing actually works and deeply study the content of this book, as it has everything you need to know to turn your online presence into a money making machine.

Knowing the ABC of social media marketing, having understood exactly what social media marketing is, how it works, how much it requires in terms of time, human resources and budget, is the fundamental premise for those who want to do social marketing in a professional and effective way. This is why it is important to get started by having a clear and exhaustive definition of social media marketing. Knowing the field you are moving on is the best way to avoid big mistakes, especially at the beginning stages. Whether you want to build your personal brand or are looking for resources to boost your company presence online, you cannot skip this first important step.

So, let's get started.

Social media marketing or SMM (also known as social network marketing, social marketing, and, by extension, also facebook marketing, linkedin marketing, etc...) is a branch of online marketing applied to social networks. This discipline exploits the ability of social media and web-social applications (apps) to generate interaction (engagement) and social sharing, in order to increase the visibility and notoriety of a brand, a product or service, a freelancer or a public figure. It includes activities such as the promotion and sale of particular goods and services, the generation of new business contacts (which are called "leads") and the increase in traffic to a brand's official

| website or social pages.

For promotional purposes it is good to integrate a social media marketing strategy with other forms of online marketing, such as: Search Engine Marketing (SEM), Social Media Optimization (SMO), Social Media Advertising (SMA) or Social ads, and Public digital relations or Digital Pr.
Social media marketing, together with social customer service, social selling and other branches of digital marketing, is considered a component of Social Business, since it also includes pay-per-click marketing activities.

Companies and organizations create, or connect to, "networks of individuals" (communities) that share interests and values expressed by the company on social networks. Then, they use these online communities to offer their users relevant content in various formats (mainly text, images and videos) in order to stimulate discussions around the brand.

This is the concrete expression of a very important marketing principle: when people speak about a company, that company can take advantage of the attention, no matter what people say about the company.

In fact, if managed correctly, user and customer interaction with these contents can produce loyalty and social media advocacy. Users and customers, with their "likes", "comments" and "shares" activate word of mouth online by individually involving their network (friends, fans and followers) in the discussion. If you have a company, you know how powerful word of mouth is. Now imagine how big of an impact it can have on your business, when you take it online, where there is virtually no limit on the amount of people one single individual can enter in contact with.

This greatly increases the possibility that a percentage of them ends up becoming a fan or follower of the company or the brand.

An important distinction: Social marketing or social media marketing?

Sometimes on blogs, podcasts and other online content, social marketing is mistakenly used as a synonym for social media marketing. In reality, social marketing is a popular discipline that became famous in the early 1970s thanks to Philip Kotler and Gerald Zaltman. When we are talking about social marketing, the "product" to be promoted is not a good or a service but is "human behavior". The goal of a social advertising campaign is in fact, for example, to encourage people to protect the environment or to fight against racism.

It is just a simple distinction, but it is important to keep this in mind as in this book we are always referring to social media marketing, not social marketing.

Chapter 2 - Advantages and Disadvantages of Social Media Marketing

Now that we have discussed and understood the definition of social media marketing, let's try to understand what benefits it can bring to a company or a personal brand. Here is a list of the main reasons why social media marketing is one of the greatest tools available to anyone that wants to do business online.

- Improvement of customer satisfaction. It has been proven that clients that can get in contact with the brand behind their favourite product are more likely to report a positive shopping experience and become returning customers.

- Increase in customer loyalty (brand loyalty). As mentioned above, people that can see a powerful online presence tend to deem that brand as "solid" and "reliable", which inevitably translates to more money for the company.

- Customer service improvement. Having a good social media presence can help a brand to give a better customer service to its clients by answering their questions directly on the different platforms. Furthermore, this behaviour improves the reliability of the company and helps people that are on the fence to become paying customers.

- Increase in sales leads and sales. As we will see in the coming chapters, social media marketing can be used to actively increase the number of leads and sales, thanks to online advertising tools.

- Increase in web traffic to the company site or personal blog. This is easy to understand. When you attract the attention of someone, you can redirect that attention wherever you want. Your or your company website is a good choice in most cases.

- Better positioning of your sitei on search engines. This is closely connected with the previous point. When you direct the attention you attract on social media to a website, that website becomes more interesting for Google and other search engines. Therefore, it is not a surprise that social media marketing is also a great way to increase the organic reach of the brand website.

- Increase in brand awareness. This really needs no comment. Brand awareness, as we will see in the coming chapters, is extremely important in this day and age.

- Connection and development of interactive relationships with your target audience. Being able to engage with your target audience is truly an incredible gift, as it allows you to better understand your customers' needs and satisfy them with your amazing product or service.

- Development of a reputation as an expert or leader in the relevant sector (brand authority). By improving your social presence, you improve the view that the general public has of your brand. Think about Apple or Tesla: they have an amazing social presence and they are considered by everyone the leader in their sector.

But is it all sunshines and rainbows?

Well, that could not be farther from the truth. In fact, social media marketing also presents some difficulties to the newcomers, but they are all manageable with the right skills. Before diving deeper, we would like to point out some point of resistance that you or your brand may face when getting started.

- Lack of resources. Social networks are varied and different, consequently the various forms of content (text, video, podcast, webinar, etc.) that have to be published and shared must be adapted to the specificities of each one of them. Likewise, a social media marketing campaign cannot be launched and left alone. It requires time and human resources dedicated to it, in order to be profitable in the long run.

  This is the reason why, at a certain point, especially for many small companies and personal brands, social media marketing becomes too expensive. By continuing reading this book you will understand how you can reduce the costs, while still building an impactful online presence.

- Negative feedback from your customers. When we

discussed the advantages of social media marketing, we stated that word of mouth is an amazing tool to boost sales. Well, that is true if people are talking positively about you. The opposite effect comes when people start giving bad feedback. This can escalate quickly and can lead to a substantial loss of users or clients.

You can avoid this in many ways, but the best one is to have a truly amazing product.

Chapter 3 - The Importance of Social Media Marketing

So, we have now come to the most important question of them all. Why should a company or personal brand invest in social media marketing? Let's discuss some points together.

- Low costs. Creating profiles on social networks is free as well as creating and managing social media campaigns with your own social media management team.

- High ROI (return on investment) from advertising costs. The ROI generated by social media advertising is the highest among the various forms of paid advertising. Furthermore, social ads are a type of advertising that allows for high target profiling and personalization. This means that the ads will only be shown to users who are really interested in products or services promoted by the advertiser. This is crucial, as it allows you to cut out everyone that is not in target with what you are offering.

- High conversion rate (CR). More than 51% of social media marketers say that developing meaningful relationships with customers has a positive impact on sales results. This inevitably increases the conversion rate of advertising.

- Improvement of customer insights. Unlike content shared through private channels such as e-mails, instant messaging tools and apps, which are therefore difficult to measure, various social media marketing tools allow precise monitoring of activities on various social networks. From the analysis of the numerous data collected (insight) using tools such as Google Analytics, it is possible to obtain important information on the "sentiment" towards the brand, as well as on the demographic composition, interests, behaviors and needs of customers.

The importance of Social Media Marketing for businesses and personal brands

Why is social media marketing important? Social networks

have become a virtual meeting place for people, where:

- they exchange ideas on the most disparate topics.
- they read reviews on products and services they want to buy.
- they look for information on places they want to go, such as restaurants or hotels.

Once, when these social platforms did not exist, this exchange of news took place in clubs or in other social gathering spaces. Today, however, people spend much more time on Instagram, Facebook, YouTube or LinkedIn and that is where they often "meet" and talk to each other. What does this mean? This means that companies and professionals should increasingly work on the ability to intercept and engage users in discussions on online social networks, because in these online environments it is possible to make them become their customers. People's opinions are increasingly influenced by conversations on the internet and this is a fact to take into account if you are selling a product on the web, if you are marketing online, or even if you just want to become important and relevant as an influencer.

Why does this trend affect us? If you are a businessman, or

an online marketer, to reach your audience - which is your potential customer base - you must become good at getting noticed where they can find you. And by now you should have understood that that place is online. You must be present and be able to influence the opinions of those who have to make purchasing decisions and you have to do that online, because it is there that purchasing decisions are made more and more frequently.

Chapter 4 - Social Media Marketing as a Career

If you are not an entrepreneur that wants to take their company online, but you are just starting to look at social media marketing as a career opportunity, just know that being proficient on social media is also important for those looking for new professional opportunities. This will help you to:

- find a job in a fresh and up to date company;
- be desired by businesses all around the world. In fact, the internet has destroyed physical boundaries and companies look for talents from all around the world, thanks to the possibility given by smart working;
- have career opportunities and increasing earnings. You have to know that social media managers are paid very well, especially if they can provide concrete results to the company they are working for.

To be interesting and attractive to companies, it will also be appropriate to become good at handling the different software, tools and platforms through which you can reach users interested in a product or service on social networks.

Who is the social media marketer?

The Social media marketer (or social media manager) is a digital marketing professional who manages and supervises the social media, digital media and social network channels within a company and acts as a connection between a community of users and the company itself.

He is also responsible for designing the content strategy, managing social media marketing campaigns on Facebook, Twitter and other social networks with the help of the social media team; the creation of an editorial plan with a view to seo; the promotion of products, services and events, and sharing the contents of the company website or blog. In small and medium-sized businesses, the role of the social media marketer is delegated to figures usually subordinate to him such as:

- Web Content Editor
- Community Manager
- Social Media Specialist
- Digital Marketing Manager
- Digital PR Manager

- Social media strategist
- Facebook Ads Specialist
- Social Customer Care Specialist

Chapter 5 - Social Media Marketing in 7 Steps

There are various ways in which a company or organization can do social media marketing. However, all social media marketing activities carried out to be effective cannot be separated from the implementation of an effective social media marketing strategy. But how to define and set up a successful social media marketing strategy?

As in any digital marketing strategy, this is developed through the definition of a social media marketing plan which consists of some precise phases. Let's take a closer look at each one of them.

Please, note that this chapter serves a general structure for the key concept that will be discussed later on in the book.

Step 1 - Conducting a social media marketing audit

In this first step, the audit activity is aimed at evaluating the digital assets (blog, site, app, etc.) available, also in relation to the competition, in order to detect on each social channel what works and what does not work.

In order to simplify this process, here is a list of a few questions that you should aim to answer in this first step. Be as precise as possible, as it will dictate the fundamental aspects of your social media marketing strategy.

- On which social platforms is the brand currently active?
- Which social networks carry the most value?
- What kind of content do competitors post?
- What tone of voice did they choose?
- How much traffic to the website does each social channel bring?
- What types of content do we post on the different channels? How frequently?
- Are we getting results from investing in social media advertising?

Step 2 - Definition of your social media marketing goals

Having analyzed the digital assets, audience and competition, the next step in establishing an effective social media strategy concerns the definition of goals and results that you hope to achieve (number of leads, customer loyalty, increased sales, brand awareness, etc.)

These goals need to be aligned with the overall communication and marketing strategy so that social media enables the achievement of business goals. In setting goals, to ensure that these will be achieved, it is good to follow the SMART method (specific, measurable, feasible, realistic, as a function of time) used for the first time by Drucker in 1954, in the book "The practice of Management" .

Step 3 - Identification of your target audience

You need to be clear who your target audience is so that the message you want to convey on social media is effective. Developing typical customer profiles (buyer personas) is essential for the development of a social media marketing strategy. The collection and analysis of data on the web or from conducting online surveys allow the marketer to paint a well rounded profile of the typical customer. Once the audience has been defined, through surveying activities, they can understand on which social platforms the customer (real or potential) is present.

How do you define your target audience?
We have a dedicated chapter in this book, but let's get a simple idea in order to better understand phase 4.
The surveying activity can be carried out with the help of some social media monitoring tools for marketing automation or manually. Let's briefly see with this last method how to do surveying on Facebook, Twitter and LinkedIn:

1. Write down a list of keywords that are meaningful to you that indicate your product, service, brand or need that you can satisfy.
2. Enter the chosen keyword in the search field of the social network and wait for the results. In the search box you can filter them by "main results", "people", "pages", "places", "groups", "applications" and

"events".

3. Enter the following data relating to the comments obtained (date, author, influence, sentiment) in an excel file and store it. This will give you an overview of what is being said online about the chosen brand or topic.

Step 4 - Creating a social media content strategy

Contents are very important in order to create engagement and to achieve your social media marketing goals. With this in mind, it is essential to follow a strategic approach focused on the creation and distribution of relevant and valuable content (Content Marketing), aimed at a clearly defined audience. This is why it is important to do step 3 before starting to produce content without a target audience in mind.

For the communication strategy on the various social media to be effective, however, it will be good to plan the management of these contents. This process is called content strategy and it requires an editorial plan.

For the planning of the editorial plan it can be useful to draw up a matrix of the contents or to use the 80/20 rule of Pareto.

In the latter case, 80% of the posts must be used to inform, train or entertain their audience, while the remaining 20% to promote the brand. As for the frequency of publication, given that quality beats quantity, for a small company 2 or 3 weekly contents are generally sufficient. Here are some of the most popular types of content:

- Infographics
- Articles
- Images
- Videos
- Ebooks
- Interviews
- Institutional or corporate news announcements
- Live and virtual events
- Assistance (customer care)

Step 5: Pay attention to Influencers

Research carried out on Twitter shows that 49% of consumers rely on the advice of Influencers in making purchasing decisions. Finding those who have a large social following for recommendations on the products or services you sell is therefore very important for the success of your social media marketing strategy. One way for a company to gain visibility with social influencers is to use the sharing system suggested by Joe Pulizzi and the Content Marketing Institute, known as Social Media 4-1-1. For every 6 content shared via social media, 4 must be relevant content for your target audience but written by influencers; 1 must be original content created by us; 1 content must be about the sale of your product or service (a coupon for example). You can see how Joe Pulizzi agrees with the Pareto Principle as well.

To engage influencers, I invite you to also take into account any affiliate program to propose to those who are part of your niche. Affiliate marketing, in fact, provides for the payment of a commission to an intermediary, in this case the influencer, for each sale or lead that it manages to generate among its audience. This translates into a win-win situation. The influencer is happy because he can get a portion of the revenues generated and the company is happy because it can get sales without spending money.

Step 6 - Choosing the social media marketing platform

A social media marketing strategy must also be planned

taking into account the market in which the company operates (B2B or B2C), the purchasing decision-making phase (social consumer decision journey) in which the customer may possibly be found (research, consideration, decision). Knowing the differences between the platforms and identifying the best ones to support the company's marketing objectives is fundamental. So let's take a brief look at the most famous social networks, not focusing on what these social media are, but in relation to the marketing activities that can be implemented with them.

Facebook

With almost 2.1 billion users and a growth of 15% (year-on-year figure), it is one of the largest social networks in the world. With this social platform it is possible to precisely identify your target audience, create engagement starting from Facebook Groups, easily implement real alternative advertising campaigns to Adwords. The possibility of integrating content in various formats into Facebook is endless and recently it is also possible by clicking on a special button to integrate Instagram content. Users of MailChimp, an email marketing software, can then natively create Facebook ads from their account.

Facebook has many arrows in its bow (Facebook media, Facebook business manager, Facebook live, Facebook connect, Facebook Stories, Facebook news feed ads, Facebook video ads). Let's briefly see the characteristics of some of them:

- Facebook Ads. Advertising on Facebook allows you to reach a conversion rate of 30% higher than other social platforms and allows a decrease in costs per conversion of 50%

- Facebook Places. Is the Facebook geo-location service that allows the user to add information about the place where he is, and based on this, find places, information of interest divided by category (restaurants, shops, entertainment, etc.) and friends who are nearby. The presence of "tiles" or boxes that refer to company fan pages make it a valuable tool for social media marketing activities.

- Facebook media. It is a tool used to teach users who have created fan pages on Facebook to manage them effectively. To access Facebook media just connect to media.fb.com.

- Facebook bluetooth beacons. The social network provides devices applicable to a physical area of your business (beacons) that allow you to send marketing communications (promotional offers, etc.) via smartphone to potential customers who pass in your vicinity. To request beacons, you must register on their waiting list.

- Facebook business manager. Is a free and easy to use tool for advertising and marketing on Facebook. From its dashboard it is possible to monitor the performance of anything connected to your business on Facebook.

Another particularity offered by Facebook is the possibility given to marketers to create effective advertising campaigns aimed at a relatively small audience through Dark Marketing activities. Through a Chrome app (Power Editor) it is possible to create "dark posts" on Facebook. In short, Facebook gives advertisers the ability to create sponsored posts that do not appear on the user's timeline but are accessible to anyone with a direct link or by clicking from an ad.

Instagram

Instagram is a photo sharing application for iPhone, Android and Windows platforms. At the heart of Instagram social media marketing are Instagram stories. They are a way to share photos and videos with your followers that will no longer be visible after 24 hours. Instagram lends itself a lot to social web marketing: people post images and videos, tag friends, insert hashtags and click on content shared by others, making Instagram the social network with the highest engagement rate.

On Instagram it is also possible to post a new type of post called "shoppable post" which includes a special tag that connects the objects in the photo directly to the corresponding e-commerce. Instagram is now testing a new "nametags" feature similar to Snapchat's Snapcodes or Messenger code that makes it easier to acquire Instagram followers. Its "visual" features make this social network suitable for b2b social media marketing, such as travel business, e-commerce and social events.

LinkedIn

LinkedIn is one of the best professional social platforms to connect with your network of collaborators (Linkedin groups) and potential future employers. The social network allows users to import contacts and integrates services such as SlideShare and Pulse. Today LinkedIn is the most popular social network for professionals in the world and is considered the most effective B2B social media marketing and lead generation platform. Like other social platforms, also on Linkedin it is possible to manage advertisements (Linkedin ads). The platform also offers businesses and publishers the ability to natively run video ad campaigns and include videos within their company pages. Through the implemented Linkedin Tracking pixel, it is then possible to measure the number of leads, sign-ups, visits to websites and other actions generated by video ads.

Snapchat

Snapchat is a mobile application that allows users to send photos and videos to friends. Snapchat Stories (collages of photos and videos shared for no more than 24 hours) are a great engagement tool. With the release of the new version of the app, it will soon be possible to share Snapchat stories also on Facebook and Twitter. Snapchat is testing new in-app e-commerce options through its Snap store located within the Discover platform, which could lead to partnerships with companies of all kinds in the future. If your products are aimed at a very young audience, marketing on Snapchat is definitely the right choice.

Pinterest

Pinterest is a popular photo sharing service that allows anyone to create collections and more. 93% of its users use it to plan purchases or to research product information. Marketing activities are possible thanks to Pinterest ads and buyable pins. Pinterest is continuing to grow among small and medium enterprises. The adhesions to its Pinterest Propel program in fact recorded a + 50% this year. With 81% of its 150 million monthly active users being women, topics such as interior design, decoration, cooking and clothing work very well.

Reddit

Reddit is the social network where the community decides what will be more relevant and what to give more visibility to. Reddit has a subreddit (think of it as a digital board) for almost every category. The growth of this social network in the world is due to 2 factors: the AMAs format (ask me everything) and the peculiarities of the voting system.

Marketing activities are possible thanks to Reddit ads, however, it is necessary to pay close attention to the large number of comments received and therefore it requires constant attention.

Telegram

Telegram is a messaging application that allows you to chat with contacts, organizing public and private groups, with a series of functions dedicated to visual content. You can add images, emojis, documents, files and links to messages. Companies can use Telegram to notify their clients of new offers and promotions or to directly chat with them if we are talking about a small and close community.

Tumblr

Tumblr is a microblogging platform with social networking features. Much used by fashion brands, bloggers and designers for the publication of very accurate content. People spend more time on this platform than on Facebook, which makes Tumblr a good place to post and advertise.

Twitter

Twitter is another fantastic social media platform that allows users to quickly send 280-character posts through Tweets.

These are characterized by the presence in the text of an hashtag (a keyword preceded by the hash symbol #). Twitter marketing is often used by companies to maintain contact with their customers, to promote their brands, products or services, and to obtain information from consumers.

Whatsapp

Whatsapp is one of the most used instant messaging applications in the world given the ease of use and quality of service. In 2017 WhatsApp crossed the milestone of 1 billion users per day, thus equaling Facebook. The app offers the possibility of interacting with your contacts within conversations and today you can publish, as status updates, temporary Snapchat-style photos and videos. With the release this year of WhatsApp Business, and the coming integration of the possibility of making payment, the brand officially accesses one-to-one marketing.

Disqus

Disqus was born as a commentary hosting service for websites and blogs. This platform now represents a real social network where users can give life to debates or participate in existing ones. To manage comments, just access the platform with the same account used for social media, using the "share" button you can then bring the discussion to your favorite social network.

YouTube

Youtube is a network where users post video blogs, video ads and videos of various genres. For marketers, videos are the ideal medium to share medium to long-form content and Youtube is the go to hosting place for video content.

Step 7 - Measurement and testing

It is necessary to constantly analyze the social media marketing strategies implemented to understand which has been effective and which has not. As part of a social media marketing strategy, it is necessary to decide which metrics or KPIs to use to verify whether the set goals have been achieved. Some metrics to consider to measure the success of a social media marketing strategy are the following:

- Cost per click (CPA)
- Conversion Rate
- Number of followers
- Brand mention
- Total shares

- Impressions
- Comments and engagement

Chapter 6 - Social Media Marketing Trends for 2021

Social media are dynamic by their nature and, for this reason, they are characterized by trends and communication methods that can vary over time (ever heard about social media trends). Knowing these trends can be crucial in choosing the most direct and effective social media marketing strategies. Below is a brief description of the social media marketing strategies that, as it seems, will most characterize 2021.

1. Use Tik Tok for your Social Media Marketing strategy. This social network is growing rapidly and is a must for those who want to reach users under 30, which currently represents 66% of the channel's users.

2. Social media wellness becomes essential to create engagement among users. People are gaining greater awareness of the use of social networks and the impact they have on mental health. This is why even the platforms themselves are committed to making the user experience pleasant and not very harmful. If you notice changes in the level of engagement, you should not be scared, but observe your competitors and if they suffer the same reduction you can feel comfortable. People are increasingly trying to reduce their time on social media and leverage the time they spend constructively.

3. Fake news will be limited. This is certainly excellent news and a very positive trend. The fact that fake news is on the decline does not mean that it still does not remain a problem. For those involved in social media marketing this means that the user will weigh heavily what you declare about your company and your products. So, please, maximum transparency!

4. Tightened security. Another growing trend strongly correlated to social media marketing is user security. The recent scandal involving Facebook and Cambridge Analytica is likely to further enhance this trend. The privacy protection measures for users of Social networks will have to be increasingly suitable to fight hacking, identity theft, phishing and various other security threats.

5. A more effective strategy with augmented reality

and virtual reality. Technology is taking great steps towards AR and VR and you must be able to adapt to this change. Augmented reality and virtual reality will improve not only the effectiveness of your strategy, but also the experience of your users.

6. The use of artificial intelligence will increase. The use of artificial intelligence (chatbots and virtual assistants) will increasingly allow marketers to interact with consumers in real time and in a personalized way. Facebook is preparing to relaunch a virtual assistant that will be able to offer suggestions to users and answer all their requests through the Facebook Messenger chat. According to Gartner, a world-leading multinational company in strategy consulting, research and analysis in the field of Information Technology (IT), 20% of business content could be generated this year by machines similar to artificial intelligence. Think about it, of every ten articles you read online, two of them are probably written by a robot.

7. Designing the social media marketing strategy to involve Generation Z. The generation of the future is becoming more and more involved with technology and this requires innovation and creativity from marketers. 2021 will be the year of the challenge to find new ways to entertain and involve the youngest, studying them carefully and understanding their needs.

8. Influencer Marketing. Social media influencers are able to generate a return on investment 11 times greater than any other digital marketing strategy. It is no coincidence that 94% of social media marketers claim to have achieved excellent results thanks to their collaboration and consider them an integral part of their social media marketing strategy.

In recent years, this tactic has been used in many sectors (social media marketing for tourism is an example above all), with results such as to become the main digital channel for many companies. The success and evolution of this tactic has also favored the creation of numerous new professional figures. Among the most sought after we find the social media marketer.

Chapter 7 - SMART Method for Goal Setting

Here is a quick overview of the SMART method.

Specific, measurable, attainable, realistic and time effective: this is how goals should be formulated, so that they are effective for the purposes of our planning and organization work. Use the SMART method for formulating goals. In this way, all the criteria that a well-formulated goal must possess will be respected.

The aim is to create an exceptional planning and organization process. Knowing what we want to achieve with our social media marketing strategy is important, but how do we state that clearly so that we can increase the odds of actually achieving our goals?

This is where the SMART method comes into place. As mentioned before, SMART is an acronym and indicates the criteria for the formulation of a goal, which must therefore be specific, measurable, attainable, realistic and have a specific time period.

Specific goals

We often make the first mistake by not reflecting deeply on what we want to achieve with our social media marketing strategy and we favor an inadequately specific formulation of our goals.

Examples of non-specific objectives:
"We want to make more money."
"We want more followers."

What do these statements mean? When is it "in the future"? And how much would you like to increase the number of followers? What does it mean to make more money? Does it refer to sales or profit? Neither objective specifies what the final perspective is. Take this into account when formulating your goal.

The same goals formulated specifically:
"In the next month, we want to increase our monthly revenue by 5% using social media marketing"
"In the next month, we will get at least 1000 more followers on our Instagram page."

Measurable goals
In order to verify the achievement of the goal or to get

motivated to work towards it, the goal must be measurable.

Examples of non-measurable goals:
"We want to post beautiful images on our social media pages."
"We want to have good comments on our posts."

What does beautiful images mean? When do you deem a comment as good? Do not leave room for interpretation. Formulate the goal in such a way that it can be verified whether it has been achieved or not.

Examples of measurable goals:
"We want to post images on social media pages that get at least 1000 likes."
"We want to receive one positive feedback every two customers."

Attainable goals

In order not to give up on your goals, it is necessary that you recognize them as such and accept it. In other words: the goal must be attractive to your or your company eyes.

Examples of unattainable goals:

"During the week we will post 100 times per day."
"In the future, all customer inquiries will be dealt with immediately."

Be honest with yourself. Can you accept these goals? Will they be attractive enough to your eyes even over a period of months? Set goals in such a way that for you personally and for all employees they are actually achievable and remain attractive over time.

Examples of attainable goals:
"We dedicate myself to our social channels consistently, posting at least 5 times per day to create brand awareness."
"All customer inquiries will be processed within 48 hours."

Realistic goals

In the throes of ambition, we have the feeling of being able to achieve anything. But even then, be honest with yourself. Are you able and are you willing to achieve these goals and keep chipping at them?

Examples of unrealistic goals:
"At the end of the day we always respond to all the comments we received that day."

"From now on we will always refund our customers."

Don't be fooled by your ambition when formulating goals. Stay realistic to avoid bankruptcy in the short term.

Examples of realistic goals:
"We organize our comment according to priorities (1 = urgent / 2 = to be fulfilled within 2 days / 3 = to be fulfilled by the end of the week) and we make sure that at the end of the day we have carried out the tasks of priority 1."
"We will refund customers that actually are suitable for the refund, based on the contract they signed when they made the purchase."

Time effective goals
Don't leave the deadline of your goal to chance.

Examples of non time effective goals:
"We will post on our social channels."
"We will answer those comments."

You now have unlimited time to do those two things. Sooner or later these goals will be reached. However, you prefer to define in the goal itself the deadline by which you want to reach it or put it into practice:

Examples of time effective goals:
"We will post on our social channels by 9am every day."
"We will answer those comments before lunch."

Think about the SMART method the next time you formulate goals for your social media marketing strategy and write them down. In this way it will be easier for you not to lose sight of them and to achieve them faster.

Chapter 8 - Pareto Principle and the Yerkes and Dodson Curve

The Pareto principle is also called the "80/20 law" or the "Pareto effect". Regardless of how you decide to call it, the principle is named after its discoverer Vilfredo Pareto (1848-1923). At the beginning of the 20th century, Pareto, an engineer, sociologist and economist, conducted research concerning the subdivision of popular heritage in Italy. Pareto's research showed that one fifth, or 20% of Italian citizens, had about 80% of the national wealth.

Pareto therefore deduced that the banks should have concentrated on that 20% of Italians to be more efficient and obtain greater profits, thus indirectly establishing that the banks only devote a fifth of their time to assisting the remaining 80% of the population.

The Pareto principle represented the inequality of the division and the lack of balance between the resources used and profit. However, this proportion was also true in other sectors.

- Commerce: 20% of products or customers invoice 80% of earnings.
- Storage: 20% of products take up 80% of the places on the shelves.
- Internet: 80% of data traffic is generated on 20% of websites.
- Road transport: 80% of all journeys take place on 20% of roads.
- Phone calls: 80% of calls are made to and from 20% of the saved contacts

The 80/20 law is best known for its application in time management. Because with a correct setting of your time it is possible to do 80% of the work in 20% of the time taken.

The goal of the rule discovered by Pareto is to achieve the greatest result with the least effort, since a lot of time is often invested in tasks with lower priority. With the right priorities and better time management, however, you can set up your work more efficiently and in a targeted manner. The Pareto principle is particularly suitable for those professional sectors with tight deadlines, allowing you to focus your efforts in the most efficient way possible and to complete the tasks within the established time frame. This 80/20 law is usually associated with other methods of time management, such as the Eisenhower principle.

There are some types of errors that are often encountered in the application of the principle in question. The first is that it is wrongly claimed that with 20% of the time invested, 80% more than normal is reached, thus bringing the yield to 100%. This is clearly a misinterpretation, where the figures are added together, thus leading to 100%, despite the fact that they are actually two different and separate aspects. Commitment and performance are not the same thing and therefore cannot be added together so easily. To generate 100% of the yield you need to commit 100% and that is especially true when it comes to social media marketing.

An interpretation of this type serves no other purpose than to give false hopes, which are far too optimistic. However, understanding the functioning of the basic principle is not enough to avoid misinterpreting its use. In fact, one might be led to think, always wrongly, that it is enough to reduce all tasks to only 20%. But here too, we must not get confused: many of the jobs that need to be done in social media marketing do not lead directly to the goal, however they are necessary to get there. Writing and replying to emails fall within the duties of this type, which in fact, although they may seem a negligible element and of little relevance to the success of a company, are nevertheless essential.

The Pareto principle serves precisely to optimize those tasks that remain necessary despite generating less or no profit, so as to take away as little time as possible. Any incorrect use of the Pareto principle can lead to the attribution of too low importance to a large part of the work to be carried out. The fact is that only those who dedicate themselves to their work in a conscious, concentrated and structured manner can obtain 80% of the results with 20% of the work done. Social media marketing falls perfectly under this principle.

The 80/20 law is very versatile. It can be used in one's private life, in study and at work for better time management. In our case, we use it to develop a much more effective and time saving social media marketing strategy. The important thing is to know which activity contributes most to achieving what you want, so as to be able to give the right priority to the various tasks. The Pareto principle helps to make the best choice in this regard.

From a purely theoretical point of view, the Pareto principle can be applied in any sector, not only in social media marketing. It has seen successful application in school and academic training, as well as in everyday life for normal people. Often the 80/20 law is associated with the working life, where it is more usual to have strict deadlines and well defined goals. But even in everyday private life there are many tasks that must be carried out in a short time and as efficiently as possible.

An example for everyday life
In order to understand the importance of Pareto Principle for social media marketing optimization, it can be useful to take a look at a common everyday life scenario.

If friends or family tell you that they will be visiting you shortly, there is little time left to clean up the house. Normally, to put everything in order and carry out all the household chores, it usually takes three hours, but in the case of such a visit, it often takes no more than an hour and a half. For this reason, following what is determined by the Pareto principle, it is initially advisable to focus on those that contribute to the well-being of the guests. Collecting objects and clothes around the apartment, putting dirty dishes in the dishwasher and cleaning the table is part of these chores.

The rooms most often used by guests are the living room, bathroom and dining room, and are therefore the ones on which you need to focus initially. Cleaning these rooms practically corresponds to the aforementioned 80% of "success", while one's bedroom, cellar and the like alter the mood of guests to a lesser extent.

In social media marketing this translates, for instance, into taking care of the most important customer requests first, prioritizing them over the less urgent ones.

Yerkes and Dodson curve
Similarly to the Pareto principle, Yerkes and Dodson law also has to do with the relationship between commitment and productivity. The curve in question takes its name from psychologists Robert Yerkes and John Dodson. From their research it emerged that productivity improves proportionally according to the growth of the commitment, at least until the maximum point is reached, or the point where the improvement in performance reaches its maximum, thus leading to a decrease in productivity.

The Yerkes and Dodson curve is represented by an inverted

U. Despite continuing to invest time and energy, productivity inevitably begins to decline once the top is reached. The high pressure and the resulting stress cause a decrease in performance, leading to worse results. Like the Pareto Principle, the Yerkes and Dodson law also affirms, or rather confirms, that only a certain part of the commitment leads to most of the productivity. The remaining effort required to achieve 100% results leads to very little in terms of productivity.

Chapter 9 - Identify the Correct Buyer Persona

As for every concept we introduce in this book, let's start by giving a detailed definition of what a buyer persona is and what it is not.

> *Buyer personas are fictitious representations of typical customers of a company, created on the basis of data collected through surveys or interviews, taking into account not only their socio-demographic, psychographic and behavioral characteristics but also data, quotes and sayings that can be useful for creating ad hoc products and services.*

These are archetypes or models that result from insights provided by consumers and users. Making use of buyer personas therefore means starting from the study of real customers to guide business and marketing strategies that will lead to the involvement, conversion and loyalty of new buyers. The insights collected may concern various types of data, such as personal information, expressions used, ways of speaking and quotes, taken during interviews, which allow us to illustrate in a more "human" way, thus going beyond the numbers and statistics relating to purchases and preferences, the "type" of person who visits a site, page or shop.

All the information collected and analyzed makes it possible to create archetypes from which brands can align their marketing strategy and brand positioning based, therefore, on the expectations of current customers and potential buyers.

The identification of buyer personas includes the collection and analysis of socio-demographic data, data relating to purchasing habits, payment methods, and much more. These are in fact useful information but not exhaustive if you intend to accurately identify the customer or the typical user of a business. As many expert explain, very often when we try to identify the target we mainly think about a demographic target. Maybe we think about the gender, the age group, the geographical area which our users come from. The reality of the facts is that what works in terms of communication is not so much knowing this information but what the behavioral and motivational data of the macro-groups and segments of users who arrive on our site are.

Knowing what their problems are and how they would like to solve them is useful, as it allows us to collect data relating to the value system of users or customers in order to create targeted content that meets their way of thinking and to conceive of reality.

The use of the term personas, intended as the creation of typical profiles of users who visit a website, is attributed to Alan Cooper, software designer and programmer who, thanks to his experience in the field, has developed and studied over the years the application of this methodology to the design sector for the creation of user-friendly software. The result of these researches was initially published in 1998 in "The Inmates Are Running the Asylum", a book that introduced the concept which then spread widely in various sectors.

The reason behind the construction of a buyer persona

These profiles are useful for guiding the decision-making process relating to multiple aspects of the business, such as the creation and definition of the characteristics of products, services and store, the definition of the structure and layout of a site, as well as marketing strategies. Furthermore, they help identify the correct brand positioning to be adopted to communicate our services and products in an appropriate manner to the various customer groups.

The traditional approach of identifying the target of a product, service or message is based on the collection of mainly quantitative data, obtained thanks to statistical analysis and socio-demographic information, but also related to purchasing behavior and preferences by channel communication.

However, this type of survey is not enough to identify the psychological nuances of the average customer or user of a site, as many marketing experts have explained during the years. In fact, as the expert explains, even if the definition of the target is essential to understand what to focus the company resources on and to identify the aspects of the business that need to be optimized, this only allows to clarify " what" to propose, but not "how" to offer it to customers. In fact, in planning a marketing strategy it is necessary to create content aimed at the different targets of the business, since a generalist and not very personalized communication cannot be in line with the way of communicating and reasoning of different customers and, therefore, it will be difficult to respond. to different doubts, worries and needs.

To better understand your target and create content that is truly relevant to potential customers, it is advisable to think like them and try to identify with the different buyer personas and their "thought structures" as David Meerman Scott explains in the aforementioned book. In the same book, the author explained that "the idea behind the concept of buyer personas is to understand your target so well that you practically start to think like him".

Design the perfect buyer persona for your company
The creation of these archetypes allows us to understand who the customers or users of a site are, but also the way they think, what they want to achieve and what are the objectives and reasons that guide their behavior, in addition to the methods and timing of purchase. To construct the identikit of the ideal customer or user, it is necessary to take into account different types of information relating to consumers and proceed with the collection of data through survey tools that allow you to listen to customers and then, in a subsequent phase, process the data that will allow to identify and construct the different buyer personas in an accurate and detailed way.

What data to collect

In the collection of data for the construction of the representations of the customer or the ideal user of a site, we range from the most personal information (such as socio-demographic, psychographic data, etc.) to those that instead relate more specifically to any response, approach or preference of the typical customer towards a product, a site or a company.

Socio-demographic data

Socio-demographic data allow you to "empathize" with buyer personas, giving them a human form, a face and an identity. Therefore, we are talking about information such as age, sex, origin, level of education, employment and income, as well as data relating to marital status, the number of children and the family unit. It is no coincidence, then, that Meerman Scott recommends giving a name to the buyer personas, precisely because these types of data allow you to "humanize" your company and related marketing strategies. Establishing that, for example, we must turn to Jane, a 37-year-old woman from New York, with more than one child and happily married, is useful to make the image that professionals have of a specific target group less abstract. This will simplify and identify the correct way they must address the communication of the brand or product.

In some cases, it may also be crucial to know the skills of the customer or typical user of our site. For example, the development of the design of a site or software or the versions of a site in different languages may vary depending on the target who in fact may be particularly familiar with those tools or may instead be a beginner. The same thing is true for linguistic skills. You have to ask yourself if a specific target group on the site knows the English language or if it is necessary to create a version in other languages as well. This, in particular, is something to be taken into consideration very seriously, especially in this multiethnic world.

Psychographic data

To understand how a certain type of customer thinks, it is also necessary to carry out a psychographic analysis, taking up elements that make it possible to identify some personality traits, attitudes, ways of thinking and typical saying of a particular buyer persona. For example, it would be appropriate to understand if it is more or less extroverted, if it is impulsive (which can affect the type of purchases and the impact of advertising communications), if it is particularly emotional or more rational, if it is more or less tending to savings, etc.

In addition to the preponderant character traits, we must also ask ourselves what fears, anxieties or frustrations can be. Think of a company that produces toys and the importance of identifying the greatest concerns of parents for their children. This, however, is not enough because it is useful to understand what leads them to buy that product. For example, parents could aim to buy a more "educational" toy, asking for opinions in the store or doing online searches, while grandparents could aim to please the child, deciding to buy a toy advertised in a TV commercial, perhaps even more expensive but which can satisfy the grandson's requests. This information can be useful in making decisions regarding the characteristics of the product, the price, but also the tone of voice of the advertising messages, therefore depending on the buyer persona to whom it is addressed.

Another important aspect concerns the predominant system of values for each buyer persona, that is, what are the moral principles not to be infringed, what kind of communication or marketing action could go against the ethical principles of a specific type of consumer. In this regard, as many experts explained over the years, it is necessary to identify the values that our brand or our site must keep alive in order not to go against the moral values of the users to whom it is approaching. Why? because, if on the one hand we are quite inclined and available to a change of opinion on certain ideas or concepts when someone (such as a brand) tries to convince us of something, on the other hand there are certain principles or values to which we are not willing to give up. One thing is certain values do not change and, on the contrary, we feel a sense of disgust and anger towards those who try to transmit moral values that are different from ours. Discover the value of your ideal customers and build your social media marketing strategy on them.

Furthermore, it is necessary to take into account not only the values but also any prejudices or preconceptions, conventions and opinions that people have regarding the most varied topics that can in some way interfere with the evaluation of a product or an advertisement and must be identified. and taken into consideration.

Needs, motivations and objectives of the buyer personas
Knowing the motivations, priorities and needs that lead customers to seek a specific solution, to solve a problem, to find out about the different brands that offer a certain service

or to buy a certain product is essential to know what to focus economic efforts on identify the elements or characteristics to be highlighted in the communication of a product or brand.

On Alan Cooper's website, Kim Goodwin mentions the different types of objectives or expectations of the buyer persona that should be identified and which must affect the design of sites, products and planning of marketing strategies. The expert refers above all to life goals, such as retiring at 45. This particular goal may not be of great relevance to anyone designing a phone, but it may be useful for someone who is creating a financial planning tool.

Limits, problems and barriers to purchase
Another important element to analyze in detail is the perception that customers have of the brand or its products. Knowing the preconceptions, opinions and criticisms that consumers have to move to a given solution will allow brands to respond accordingly, proposing changes based on the various problems identified. Furthermore, once any obstacles to purchase have been identified, that is, anything that could lead a customer to decide that they no longer want to buy the

product or even try it, companies can create a communication that allows them to overcome these obstacles.

Decision criteria

What criteria do different customers or users focus on for purchasing decisions? Knowing what drives consumers to choose one brand to the detriment of another is of great importance for companies, since it allows you to understand not only what the advantages that make your product essential for a specific target are, but also the problems that make it so that it prefers the solution offered by a competitor.

Buyer journey

The analysis of the buyer journey is essential first of all to understand which are the points of contact with the company that will allow you to reach the customer effectively, inspiring trust and meeting the preferences for the use of content and research of the information. It is necessary to know the process or the path taken by customers before arriving at the purchase of the product, so as to understand what difficulties or problems there are and how to overcome them effectively.

It is therefore of great interest to obtain data on all the

obstacles that can intervene in the purchase process. How can you do this? For example, you can achieve this by asking the user the type of sources they use when looking for information on products or services and through which channels they usually receive or would prefer to receive commercial communications. Remember, if you control the journey of your customer you control your customer.

Effective tools for data collection

There are several tools that allow you to collect the information needed to build buyer personas. Social media, and therefore tools such as Facebook Audience Insights but also Google Analytics, can be very useful for collecting large amounts of demographic data, as well as the times in which each group of users is most active on the web, their geographical origin and related interests.

In addition to the processing of statistical data relating to personal data or purchasing behavior, the carrying out of interviews is particularly important because it also allows you to analyze the type of language used by the buyer personas and therefore understand the style of communication, the words, the terms that may hit them more. Therefore, it may be useful to extract from these one or more representative quotes of each buyer persona, their motivations, fears, aspirations, expectations towards brands or products but also their life goals, for example. On the basis of this information, short bibliographic descriptions can be constructed that can serve as inspiration for the creation of content aimed at that specific group of customers. You can also use online surveys sent via email through, for example, Google Form.

How to analyze the data you collect

Once the data has been collected, how to put them together to create the identities of the ideal customer or the different types of customers? As for the ideal number of buyer personas, according to David Meerman Scott, it must be identified "on the basis of the factors that differentiate them". For example, some companies may have a different profile to represent the Asian, European and North American customer, thus creating different archetypes according to the different geographical areas in which it operates. It all depends on the sector, the type of company and business you offer, as well as the different target groups involved.

Chapter 10 - Content Strategy: Everything You Need to Know

Content strategy and content marketing are often confused and used as synonyms, but they are and remain well-defined elements with the first being hierarchically superior to the second. In fact, we will see how a content strategy can exist without even a glimpse of content marketing. Because "content is king" remains a valid dogma, but there is no king without a kingdom that has precise borders within which to exercise its hegemony.

Before diving deeper into content marketing, it is important to give a definition of what we are talking about and distinguish content marketing from content strategy.

Content marketing - definition
Content marketing is the creation and dissemination of useful and valuable content, aimed at a well-defined audience, with the aim of attracting it, acquiring it and inducing potential customers to take profitable actions.

Content strategy - definition

Content strategy deals with the planning aspects of content management throughout its life cycle. It includes the analysis phase, the alignment of the content with the business goals, influencing its development, production, presentation, evaluation, measurement and archiving. What the content strategy is not, however, is the content implementation phase. Practical development, management and dissemination of content are the tactical results of the strategy, what needs to be done for the strategy to be effective.

Thus, Rahel Anne Bailie, a famous content strategis, in an article on her blog dated 2009 but still valuable, stated this exact difference.

Basically, the two phases are split. The first one involves strategic planning and the second one, which is subsequent and regulated by the first, involves the creation and share of the content in its different forms.

Content strategy is what lies upstream, it is the planning activity that defines and regulates this process. The difference lies in the fact that the content strategist does not deal with the production of content but turns his attention to the planning of the same, not limiting himself to defining when they should be published but above all why they should be produced. Each content, in fact, must be a single brick useful to build the bigger building. It is a work of engineering and architecture for which not only workers and concrete are needed, but first of all a clear, defined project divided into several phases. Without precise planning, clear goals to strive for and measurable objectives to be achieved, the contents will be ineffective and self-referential. They simply won't "stand up", exactly like a building built in the absence of a blueprint.

Content strategy and content curation

As evidence of how much and how the content strategy has an absolute value greater than content marketing, there are numerous examples of strategies of extraordinary success without even the production of their own content. In this case, we leverage on content curation (defined as the ability to filter and add value to the contents we receive daily from all online sources, i.e. the process of selection, collection, organization and subsequent sharing of content relating to a particular topic or subject area).

We can offer useful content to potential customers that are simultaneously in line with our business goals. We are referring to reporting, commenting and rewriting articles written by third parties that thus enter the information sphere of our audience. In this way, we will add a valuable contribution capable of underlining our expertise in the field, the relevance of the subject for our industry and the usefulness of that information for those who receive it.

Structuring a winning content strategy

In a broader marketing action, whether it is inbound marketing or social media marketing, content remains the main focus or at least it should. In defining the strategy, a good content strategist can and must make use of numerous tools and suggestions to identify topics of interest. Among these, in addition to what a paid platform like Hubspot offers, Google offers valuable and free help. Through the Adwords keyword planner it is possible to know the search volume for the keyword that has been identified as being of interest for the target audience. Google Trends, on the other hand, allows you to measure the degree of interest of that keyword in a given period, thus knowing its variations, noticing any new trends.

However, the choice of specific topics to be treated is a step subsequent to numerous others that precede it. It will be essential to first establish what the goals of our marketing action are and which target we would like to talk to. Subsequently it will be necessary to identify a message that differentiates us from the competition and that can be the beacon of our communication. Then, thoroughly analyze the market and competitors and identify the most suitable channels to spread our messages. Finally, establish what KPIs to measure to be aware of the progress of our strategy.

Defining the goals for your content strategy in the most effective way

A content strategist is called upon to confront the objectives indicated by the companies for which he works. Often, these milestones are rather vague, complicated to quantify.

"I would like to have more visibility". Would it mean having more visitors to your site? Or, "I would like to increase sales". Ok, but on which segments? Not having a magic strategy that works for everything, you need to choose which categories of people to focus your communication on to try to increase sales in that specific area. It is therefore necessary to discuss and define the goals in advance in a precise and specific way.

It is on the basis of them, moreover, that each individual content and the entire content strategy must be oriented.

For example, "increasing sales generated from the youngest portion of our clients" could be a clear, concrete, measurable goal and referred to a specific target.

But what are the most common goals that a content strategy can aim to achieve? Here is an exhaustive list, that will give you a better idea on where to focus your attention.

• **Lead generation.** Contents and landing pages structured in such a way as to facilitate the compilation of a form through which to obtain useful information on potential customers.

• **Media and digital pr.** Our goal will be to obtain media coverage by creating news that has an organic, viral diffusion.

• **Distinctive positioning**. Our purpose will be defined by communicating what exactly the company does, positioning it precisely in that sector and distinguishing it from its competitors. This is an extremely important goal that, if achieved can lead to enormous amount of success.

• **Customer support.** Our contents will be aimed at clarifying the terms and conditions of the service, the characteristics of the products and the sales mechanisms.

• **Community building.** Our editorial plan will be aimed at creating a sense of belonging, identification towards the brand through a sharing of values that emerges from a story that is as shared as possible, horizontal, friendly.

The definition of the target of a content strategy: the buyer persona

As discussed in the previous chapter, identifying the correct buyer persona is extremely important in a social media marketing strategy.

Mapping the purchasing process and intervening at every stage with the right content, at the right time, aimed at the right person is the overall and final goal of a well rounded content strategy.

To understand if a message is interesting or not, if a content can be relevant or not, we will have to understand who should receive it. Have in mind who to turn to at every time, as this is a crucial part of every social media marketing strategy.

Identifying your audience, defining it as specifically as possible is the key to drawing up a winning content strategy. Information such as age, gender, educational qualification, for many product categories are now superfluous.

At all levels of marketing, a fall in the importance of personal data is being observed in favor of buyer personas. The modern identity of the potential customer we address is reconstructed by integrating demographic and, above all, psychographic data. This means taking into strong consideration interests, behaviors, reasons for purchasing, doubts and fears regarding our service, product or our entire industry.

In short, information that is not only useful but essential to understand in which contexts these categories of people are more accessible and inclined to listen to our message and what makes that message relevant for them. We will have a dedicated chapter on this topic later on in this book.

Identify the differential message of the content strategy

Differentiate to qualify, that is key. A winning content strategy cannot ignore the identification of a differential message, of a corporate plus value that allows us to stand out from the competition. Our differential message will be our beacon. In fact, in all our content we will have to ask ourselves if it has been underlined, or at least implied. And it must be one and only one. The customer is bombarded with numerous advertisements every time he logs in and is looking for someone who can simplify his choice by clarifying which is the best, or most immediate, for that need he wants to satisfy.

It is not enough to position yourself only for the characteristics of your product

It is necessary that these are also sought after by the market and that they are not already totally controlled by the competition. In other words, you have to trigger a need and the inability to satisfy it by your competitor. That is how you win in business.

Positioning yourself on the market for a certain category or quality allows you to differentiate yourself from others

The entire content strategy will be defined by always

referring to the added value that we guarantee and will aim to associate the brand with that distinctive feature that allows the simplest and most immediate mental association possible for the final consumer.

Market and competition analysis

We know we want to differentiate ourselves, but how can we do it if we do not have full and precise knowledge of what our competitors are doing?

Content strategy is still marketing, and marketing needs a benchmark. A comparative analysis with respect to our direct competitors is essential to trace the differences, their respective weaknesses and strengths. Without forgetting a broader investigation than what other similar companies do but outside our specific market, in order to obtain some useful ideas to integrate our content marketing plan.

Multi-channel content strategy

A multi-channel content strategy is essential. Stories and contents on the internet can branch out expanding, wandering, deepening, even through hypertext links. They can migrate between multiple platforms, channels, also passing from online to offline and vice versa. Our final consumer himself is now multi-channel, therefore multiplying the possibilities of intercepting him can only be one of our primary objectives.

We will have to do this by taking into account that each channel has its own characteristics that define it, peculiarities that must be taken into account already in the strategy definition phase, devising contents that can intercept and engage the audience that uses them.

What works for Facebook will most likely not work for LinkedIn, or Twitter and vice versa. The people reached will be different, the communication model adopted on the different platforms will be different.
Ignoring this aspect and republishing the same content on each different digital channel can only condemn our editorial plan to irrelevance.

Organic share and promoted content
A good web content editor knows he has to follow the guides provided by the content strategist on the creation and dissemination of his contents. It will also be essential, already in the drafting phase of the strategy, to define a budget to be allocated to sponsored content. Entrusting your editorial calendar to organic distribution alone could be very

limiting.

Social advertising allows us to define with extreme precision the audience we can hit. Furthermore, knowing right from the start on which categories of content to invest in order to guarantee them the necessary "push" to establish themselves and get closer to our business objectives simplifies and simplifies processes.

Chapter 11 - Content Strategies for Different Buyer Personas

In previous chapters we have discussed the importance of having a good content strategy. We have also touched on the point that there is not a better content in absolute terms, but that it depends on who consumes said content. Let's dive a bit deeper in this concept.

Creating customized content for different buyer personas is essential to engage different consumer or user groups. David Meerman Scott gives the example of the creation of a university site that must address buyer personas with very different characteristics, objectives and motivations. In this case, the site must contain pages with content suited to the needs and expectations of the various interested parties.

Demonstrating how the creation of content can vary within the same site, the expert illustrates five possible buyer personas to be developed: former students, who are contacted to convince them to make donations; high school students, worried about submitting an application for university access and who need clear and detailed information; the parents of prospective students, who will certainly look for reassuring information on where the off-site students will live; current students to be persuaded to enroll again in a master's or other course of study; a more general section with the most frequently asked questions to avoid wasting time in university offices.

Different people come to the site or shop for different reasons, they are used to a different language and expect to find a certain type of information or certain products, which is why marketers, as explained by the expert, should undertake to use the information on buyer personas to create specific marketing and PR plans to reach each one of them.

Chapter 12 - The Basics of Copywriting for Social Media Marketing

Now that we have extensively covered how to create your advertising campaign on Facebook, it is important to talk about the basics of copywriting. This skill is absolutely fundamental to take your content strategy to the next level and to improve the conversion rate of your posts and articles.

Here is the definition of copywriting.

> *Copywriting is the activity of writing advertising texts, within the broader marketing sector, with the aim of attracting and capturing the attention of the target audience so as to obtain a sale or generate a lead. Whoever writes such texts is called a copywriter.*

The results that are intended to be achieved through advertising materials can be many, but these are always and closely linked to triggering a concrete action by the user. In most cases, this action consists in a subscription or a purchase. Those who deal with copywriting, therefore, must be salesmen, to the extent that, through the use of the right written words, they manage to persuade the customer or user to take an action. For instance, buying or even responding to a call-to- action aimed at a possible future sale, through the acquisition of a lead, or a contact.

Copywriting, therefore, is not an art - as we read in many articles on the internet- it is not to the extent that the drafting of advertising texts does not convey its own interiority and the aim to be achieved is not only that of communicating and arousing emotions. The text must promote a brand and must convey, through words, specificities such as to capture the attention of users and trigger emotions that make them remember it later, when they make a purchase or in any case take an action in favor of the brand.

Copywriting is often defined as an art because of the dose of creativity that this job requires. In fact, you cannot be a copywriter without being creative, without knowing how to play with words, with their meanings, with figures of speech, without knowing how to arouse in the mind others images and concepts, even abstract ones.

Furthermore, we cannot say that copywriting is a science or that it has such scientific rigor as to lead to certain results. Copywriting, however, is a marketing activity, for which specific knowledge and an accurate strategic and analytical study of the brand's objectives, market and target audience are required, in order to aim at achieving certain results.

Approaching "scientific copywriting" means admitting that creativity is not always everything and, indeed, sometimes it must be put aside: being creative without having a method will not lead to poor results.

The texts written by a copywriter are numerous, both offline and online.

Among the offline texts are those for:

- advertisements for magazines and newspapers or billboards, in all of their components. From the headline to the body copy, slogan or claim and payoff;
- texts on the packaging, on product packages, sometimes also containing coupons to be used for subsequent purchases and invitations to collect points;
- brochures, postcards, flyers, etc;
- television and radio commercials.

Among the online texts, there are:

- newsletters and more generally texts for email marketing activities with a sales purpose;
- product sheets on eCommerce sites;
- advertisements for online platforms;
- texts that contain calls-to-action;
- banner.

Copywriting techniques

What are the most effective copywriting techniques when it comes to social media marketing?

Let's start with a consideration. The main task of the copywriter is to write ads capable of capturing the attention of the target audience.

As this is a work based on creativity, it is difficult to establish precise rules to guide the work. However, we can outline some guidelines.

First of all it is necessary to identify the target to be reached, because the message is effective only if it adopts a language suitable for the target audience. The more specific the audience, the easier it is to hit the goal.

Since the ultimate goal of a copywriting activity is to sell, the product must occupy a central position with respect to the creative idea. For this reason it is important to follow the principle of the Unique Selling Proposition (USP), that is the formulation of a single creative idea, which will have to highlight the characteristic considered most important when designing the strategy, following the indications of a brief.

Finally, contradictions must be avoided. In fact, it is essential that the image and the text say different things, so as not to overlap, but complementary, to complete each other's message. A well-set formal structure makes the ad easier to decode and allows you to get in tune with the target audience more quickly.

Once these basic concepts on copywriting are established, let's see together some simple techniques for creating effective and engaging content, especially on the web.

The first copywriting technique consists in repeating the title. When writing a copy you will have to repeat in the text the same words used in the title but combined in a different way or enriched with the addition of further information to reinforce the message. Also in the field of Search Engine Optimization this technique is very useful for communicating important information to search engine robots.

The second technique involves concreteness. The goal in this case is to attract the reader or user by focusing on a problem or interest of the user himself. Introducing concrete and measurable data and new information compared to that offered by competitors, makes the copy really attractive to the target audience.

The "problem technique" instead consists in asking a common question, to which many users seek an answer, to make them feel involved in the discussion. But be careful, because the question must be a real question and not a rhetorical question, to which everyone already knows the answer. Otherwise the risk is to frustrate the readers.

The second to last technique is the "alternative technique". After we have posed the question using the problem technique, we can also offer a concrete answer or an alternative to an already known answer, proposing ourselves as experts in our sector. In this case it is important to highlight all the features of the product or service we offer that can help the target audience to solve their problem.

The last technique is focused on a call to action. This tactic is very useful especially at the end of a text. The call-to-action encourages the user to click on an ad or interact with the brand. Users will know what to do to get the information they need and will be guided by your words in this discovery process

What persuasive copywriting is

Often, those who write online content do so to encourage readers to take an action (call-to-action). For example, to subscribe to the newsletter, leave a contact, purchase a product or service and much more. To do this, there are specific rules that take the name of persuasive copywriting.

Persuasive copywriting starts with an analysis of the characteristics of the product, even compared to competitors, and uses the right words to convince the public of the goodness of its choice.

Persuasive copywriting takes into account the needs of users, those who drive our every action. The text must be specific, describing and recounting every detail: the more exhaustive it is, the more you have the chance to convince the reader.

People need to be able to touch the product through words, just as if they were seeing it in front of their very own eyes. Persuasive writing, in fact, touches the emotions.

Most of the time people buy on impulse, following the flow of their emotions. A good copywriter knows how to strike the right chords to be able to hit this goal. For this it is necessary to know the rules of persuasive copywriting.

To arouse emotions, a good copywriter tells rather than describes. When you write to convince someone to buy something or to take an action, it is a good rule to turn the text to a positive form. Eliminate "no" and "not" from sentences, this is a simple trick that will give you many satisfactions.

People read the beginning and the end, but what is in the middle is usually skipped. Readers are distracted and on the internet are in a hurry so they pay attention to the opening sentences, then they quickly scroll through the text and read the conclusion. In light of this data, the most relevant information in the text should be inserted precisely in these sections.

Without a call to action there is no persuasive copywriting. It is unlikely that someone will perform a certain action on their own initiative. People are naturally lazy and you have to guide them through the purchase. A good call-to-action is direct, short and gives an urgent character to the reader.

A final important role in persuasive writing is that of testimonials. In fact, the positive feedback of people who have already purchased a product or service are very important, especially on the internet where things cannot be seen and cannot be touched. Word of mouth remains one of the best advertisements ever, and consumers tend to trust the reviews of other consumers more than they trust you as a business.

The last rule for persuasive copywriting is to always remember that a good text puts the people who read it at the center and from here it starts to develop the different concepts. Who are the readers? It is necessary to speak their language correctly if you want to capture their attention.

Examples of good copywriting

Copywriting, therefore, allows us to have creative and persuasive texts, which accompany different types of publications: from the blog post to the advertisement, from the tweet to the product sheet for an eCommerce, examples of copywriting are everywhere.

To better understand what we mean, we have selected three particularly successful examples, which apply copywriting to different types of text.

1. UrbanDaddy

UrbanDaddy frequently sends emails to its customers, recording high open rates, thanks to a secret ingredient. Every email UrbanDaddy sends is fun, right from the subject of the email.

The company avoids long preambles to the message, so readers don't feel like they're wasting time reading that email. The tone of voice is a mixture of the classic promotional slogan and irony, to emphasize the fun aspect of the product.

The company knows its audience and knows it can joke to grab attention.

2. Trello

If you are into social media marketing, you certainly know Trello, a very useful tool for team project management and daily task management. But perhaps you've never stopped to consider the copywriting aspect of its site.

The product description is clear and written in a very simple style. All features are listed in a single sentence that reassures the user.

The images are also integrated with an explanatory copy that allows you to immediately understand all the features and methods of use of the tool.

3. VISA

Despite being one of the most used credit cards in the world, Visa has identified an emotional distance between the brand and customers.

So the company decided to create the GoInSix campaign: a series of interactive content to motivate people to eat, shop or travel, using six-second videos, six-image cartoons or just six words.

The campaign worked on all social channels, also thanks to a particularly successful copy, based on a very familiar formula for customers: the to-do list, rethought in an emotional key.

We advise you to dig deeper into these 3 case studies as they will show you how important it can be to have a good copy.

Chapter 13 - SEO Copywriting

Now that you have understood the importance of copywriting for your ads, it is time to discover what a good copy can do for your business in terms of ranking your site on Google, the most used search engine in the world. This is where SEO copywriting comes into play.

The definition is pretty simple.

> *If copywriting is the art of writing persuasive and conversion-oriented content, SEO copywriting is the art of combining this content with search engine optimization.*

How can we not consider today the enormous possibilities offered by the Internet for every company? Impossible. And what is the best way to be found by potential customers on Google? Of course, writing relevant content - interesting and useful, capable of responding to user searches - and optimized for SEO.

A copywriter today cannot ignore the correct use of metadata and the consistent publication of content to aim for the best indexing on different search engines.

Knowing the structure of an online article, knowing how to correctly use h1, h2, meta description and keywords is essential when copywriting for the web.

Good and informative content now accounts for about 50-60% of what allows you to reach the best search engine rankings and if having good writing skills is already a skill, being able to implement SEO-optimized writing is a true double benefit.

Below you can find a list of the essential features to keep in mind to produce content from a SEO perspective.

- Use the h1 tag for the title and the h2, h3 tags, and so on for the paragraph and subparagraph titles. This helps Google to identify that your article has a well defined structure, allowing your article to rank higher.

- Use keywords in a natural way in the text and use its variants (singular and plural, synonyms, antonyms). Repetition is not seen very well by search engines, so be creative.

- Use bold, italic and underlined consistently. A well formatted article is what Google wants to ses.

- Use meta tags. These help a proper formatting of the article, keep them in mind.

- Use bulleted and numbered lists. For some reasons, Google loves lists. Try to insert them in every article or long-form post you publish.

- Rename the files and images using the keywords in the title, fill in the alternative text field.

- Use internal links and external links that are useful, consistent and relevant. Cross-references are what build the internet. It is important to insert links in every content you publish, no matter the platform, as this will give users a broader experience of your brand.

- Insert links on relevant anchor text. Of course, links have to be put in the right place. Do not paste them at the end of an article, rather hyperlink them at a proper place.

Chapter 14 - Copywriting as a Career

Like we have done in a previous chapter, in this book we want to give concrete career opportunities as well. We understand that not everyone is meant to be an entrepreneur and social media marketing offers many pathways to those that are willing to take up the challenge. Becoming a copywriter is definitely a suitable option for many. Here is more information about this.

You may have thought at the beginning of this chapter that being a copywriter is a job that anyone can do: "You just need to know how to write in English!" you might have said to yourself. But we are sure that by continuing to read you will have realized how many skills and knowledge are needed.

The way to become a judge, notary or teacher is always very clear: a degree, a few years of internship, a state exam or a qualification and if you pass all this, you are in. Obviously we are simplifying the concept here, but only to explain that to become a copywriter often the path is not so linear and defined. There are endless ways to create a professionalism that goes beyond knowing how to write well, even if the basics are the same for everyone.

First of all, you have to focus on your training. A bachelor's degree in humanities or at least some training in this field will certainly make your life easier, but you can't think that you are already a professional copywriter after publishing a few dozen articles on a blog.

Even without taking writing courses, you can start from the material you find on the internet to understand how to write quality content. Sign up on LinkedIn and Facebook groups on the subject to find opinions, suggestions and insights, and then read, read a lot, read anything, especially advertising related material.

Another useful suggestion is to start specializing immediately on a few topics, to be deepened and studied in depth, based on what your passions are, but always following lines related to the business, for which there may be companies interested in having you as a producer of their content.

Having your own blog is not essential, but it is certainly a great exercise, especially to train consistency in writing. You won't always write about what you like or when you like.

Being a job you will need to be able to develop those techniques that allow you to really do it for work.

Use Google Analytics and the Google Search Console, accompanied by other SEO tools, to refine this aspect in your articles.

During the training phase, also accept some free collaboration if the one who proposes it to you can offer you a benefit in exchange, such as a training course or simply the opportunity to mention the collaboration that is so important in your CV.

Take courses, including online ones, to specialize on specific topics and acquire new skills in Digital Marketing, SEO strategies and Social Media Marketing. You will have many more arrows in your bow than the competition by learning from the best professionals in the sector.

Becoming a copywriter depends a lot on your ability to experiment and look for different paths for your training, but you should also have some basic skills. These are the following.

- Know in depth the language in which you will write the texts: a grammatical error from a copywriter is unacceptable;

- You must like writing: don't think of becoming a copywriter just to work from home or because you imagine it to be an easy job;

- Have creativity: the copywriter is not a writer, but his ability to use the word must be close to that of an artist and the same is true for his ability to use figures of speech and turns of phrase;

- Know how to adapt: as in all freelance jobs, customers will always be different and it will be up to you to reconcile their requests with your professionalism, proposing the right tone of voice and thinking about the correct target;

- Never stop studying: even writing like the web and social media is constantly evolving and even current events can affect your texts, so, once again, read, read a lot and stay updated;

- Be patient: as we said, not all customers are the same and not everyone will always do well with your work. The important thing is to understand the goals and try to achieve them together. Varying the work until it is perfect.

Job opportunities for copywriters

Hiring a copywriter is an excellent idea for any type of business, from startups to large companies to small and medium-sized businesses.

In fact, everyone deserves quality content.

"Content is King" has become a kind of mantra in recent years, and for this reason the copywriter is becoming one of the most sought after positions in the new economy based on social interactions.

The ingredients to earn a place of preference in the arms of recruiters will naturally be transversal skills, able to range from the choice and creation of the visual aspect of the communication, to the SEO optimization of the content produced. No improvisation, then, because if even the best happen to make mistakes, precision for a copywriter will have to be one of the main directions during job interviews.

In short, for companies, hiring a copywriter is becoming increasingly essential, regardless of their size, because knowing how to say the right things in the right way gives seriousness and professionalism to the brand and offers new opportunities for contact with potential customers.

There is no shortage of job offers. Just do a simple Google search to check how many ads it is possible to find throughout your state, you will be amazed.

Depending on the experience and skills acquired, a copywriter can earn up to 5.000 dollars per month. Everything, as usual, however, depends on the companies you work with, on the projects you are committed to and on your level of professionalism.

Freelance or company copywriter?

There are several options for copywriters and aspiring copywriters: from freelance work, excellent especially at the beginning for the classic apprenticeship, to working in a company as an internal resource.

Today more and more companies are able to seize the huge opportunities of digital marketing and social media marketing and for this reason having a copywriter in the company means having a person dedicated to the production of all company texts. From copy for social channels to texts for informative materials, print, up to the content for the corporate blog, you name it: everything that requires some sort of writing is done by the copywriter.

However, the freelance solution remains the most flexible one, as a freelancer is able to guarantee autonomous organization of working times and methods, as long as it has a solid personal organizational base.

Chapter 15 - The Importance of a Company Blog

Having a corporate blog is an essential requirement for all businesses today. Please, don't commit the mistake to think that, since we have talked about social media platforms up to this point, we do not recommend having a company website. This could not be farther from the truth.

Those who decide to open and manage a corporate blog do so to promote their products and services to their target audience. But creating and managing a corporate blog isn't easy.

We imagine that you have realized this as well, if you have tried to do social media marketing before reading this book.

Probably many times you have thought about creating a blog for your company or personal brand, but you did not know where to start, or the people you turned to did not achieve the desired results. Who knows how many times you have thought that your articles do not receive visits, that users do not read your content and you have never found an answer to the reason behind this lack of results.

The management of a corporate blog is in fact a complex and very extensive activity that requires an investment in terms of both time and money.

For this reason, we would like to tell you that it must be entrusted to expert people who know how to promote specific marketing campaigns. Working in this direction means investing a lot in your business and creating corporate value for the various stakeholders. We suggest you take this approach even if you are working by yourself.

A corporate blog is neither an encyclopedia nor a box to be filled with intrusive advertising. The strategy behind a blog is to create and disseminate interesting content to your target audience. Period, end of the story.

However, putting this into practice is difficult and requires commitment and a creative effort.

What we are saying is that to open a blog you need to have a strategic plan designed ad hoc. In this chapter we are going to show you the right approach to have when considering the idea of having a blog for your company or personal brand.

Outline your business blog goals

First of all, to aspire to have a successful blog you have to understand what your goals are when you are creating it.

For this reason you will have to ask yourself specific questions:

- Why should we start a blog?
- What do we want to communicate with my blog?
- What are my ultimate goals for this blog?

Having the answers to these kinds of questions clear will allow you to start off on the right foot. Please, set the goals for your blog using the SMART method.

The importance of contents of a corporate blog

When you start writing on your business blog the first question you need to ask yourself is the following. What kind of content do we want to post?

It must be something that is easy to understand for the user, which allows him to immediately put into practice what he has read, which offers a solution or comments on an issue that is important to him and which has a link with the products and services offered by yours. company.

Each blog page must deal with a particular topic and theme related to your business, it must not contain news from other sectors or personal information since it is not a personal diary.

Publish the right amount of articles per month

You have to schedule your content, make it interesting and publish it with a certain regularity and frequency.

You can't think of having a corporate blog if you publish a post every now and then.

Try not to spend months between the publication of one post and another, but write constantly and follow a pattern. You will have to try to publish at least one post a week, especially in the first period, and you will have to make sure that those who read you expect to find your content published on that precise day, for example every Monday, Tuesday, etc.

This way you will create a routine and a fixture for readers who will be enticed to return willingly to your blog.

Choose the writer

Not everyone is good at writing, as we have seen in the chapter dedicated to copywriting.

Entrusting this task to a person who does not have the appropriate skills could be a really big mistake.

If you do not have professionals in the sector within your staff, contact the agencies that develop corporate blogs. They can create a tailor-made content marketing strategy for you. In the immense ocean of the web, there are many corporate blogs and the competition is high.

The blog is like a goldfish swimming in the ocean depths and must be found (by users) in the midst of sharks and other ferocious fish species that inhabit the seabed.

We used this metaphor to tell you that to bring more and more readers to your corporate blog, you need to worry about promoting it as well.

To gain visibility online, developing an SEO strategy is

essential.

In this way, in fact, your content will be able to rank high on search engines and be easily searchable by users. Furthermore, you should allocate a part of your budget to paid advertising to always intercept new users interested in your content.

The advantages of a business blog

Whether you run a small business or a large company operating in any sector (agriculture, industry or service), you are likely wondering if having a blog is really worth the time and effort.

The answer is definitely yes. Blogging is a relatively simple and inexpensive way to improve your marketing strategies, drive visitor traffic, and attract more customers.

Statistics from Hubspot's Inbound Marketing Report highlight how important it is to have one. In fact, according to the study, 57% of companies that have a blog reported acquiring at least one or two new customers a day.

Furthermore, about 81% of companies say that their blog is useful for supporting business activity and interacting better with consumers.

A business blog helps you make money

Creating a corporate blog is a good starting point for earning and obtaining a return on investment and, for this, it is necessary to take care of the blog on a daily basis and draw up an editorial plan before starting to post.

Although at first it can generate a monetary spend, in the medium to long term the investment will bear the desired results and will generate an excellent return on invested capital.

This is why it is important to create a blog that allows your business to take off from a reputational point of view, but above all in terms of ROI and sales volume.

Improve the SEO positioning of your blog

Search engines favor corporate websites that publish content that is updated, valuable, informative and of great added value. If you pay attention to SEO optimization, the search engines will reward you.

An important fact is the following. Blogs offer on average 434% more indexed pages and 97% more indexed links.

Remember that when you publish a blog post, SEO optimization is essential to appear high on search engines.

Increase the reputation of your company
Writing "fresh" content that is rich in advice and information helps to accomplish the following goals.

- Increase the visibility of your brand;

- Contribute to the improvement of your reputation and the good positioning of your company within the sector in which it operates;

- Outperform the competition;

- Become a leader in the industry in which you operate;

- Build loyalty with your audience;

- Build brand awareness.

In fact, every quality article is a way to communicate to customers and visitors their competence with respect to the topic and the reference sector.

You can link it to your social channels

Sharing topics and articles from the blog to social networks (Facebook, Twitter and LinkedIn) helps to increase customer engagement, brand loyalty and, consequently, monetary income.

Give a "human face" to your company

Creating a corporate blog allows you to create a "virtual" space where you can show users and customers your true spirit and philosophy of your company.

By sharing your experiences, case studies, presenting new products and evaluating industry news, customers can take a look at what is the essence of your business.

In essence, the blog gives your business a voice.

Differentiate yourself from the competition

A corporate blog helps you differentiate yourself from the competition, forces you to think about the latest trends, industry news, your customers and the world as a whole.

Blogging also helps you outperform the competition and position your company as a leader in their sector rather than a follower.

You get to know your customers

Through a blog, you have the opportunity to obtain interesting key information about your audience and actual and potential customers, by monitoring the topics that receive the most shares and comments.

You can do quality link building

The positioning of your blog on the search engine also depends on incoming links. Thanks to well-written posts and content, you can attract high quality reposts from other websites, which will allow your blog to rank even higher. It is a virtuous cycle and we suggest you take advantage of it.

Remember that quality content is important because it gives you value and with it you can improve your ranking on Google.

How to create a corporate blog that outperforms the

competition

Corporate blogs are certainly an innovative and much more effective advertising tool for one's business than ordinary and more traditional ones.

It used to be possible to advertise your business simply with an ad or a banner, but today the consumer wants more. He wants to identify with the company, he wants to know its history and also to receive useful information from it for his daily life.

The corporate blog therefore not only has an advertising function, but also serves to give the consumer exactly what he is looking for, which is a great story.

That is why it will be vital to follow some guidelines if you want to build a successful business blog. Here are few points to keep in mind.

Focus on a story

To be successful with your business blog, avoid using it as a simple advertising tool.

Instead, the blog must become a connecting channel between the company and your potential customer, or rather a collector of stories. Try to use it, therefore, to spread important news about your business, to tell something about you and your company.

Mind the style of writing

A corporate blog cannot be built without taking into consideration important elements such as the writing style and even the graphics. Writing in correct English is the basis, avoiding mistakes and excessive repetition is a must.

Try to capture the customer's attention with graphic elements that are captivating. From titles and bold, to the presence of real images and other multimedia content.

Give your customers a voice

A great way to tell a story on your business blog is to give your customers a voice.

In particular, ask them if you can tell and share their past experiences or if they themselves want to write a few lines about you.

Of course, always be honest: don't make up anything, but emphasize the positive aspects of the story you're going to tell in your post.

Observe your competitors and learn from them

You are not alone in your market, so being able to understand what your competition is doing can be a great way to improve your corporate blog even more from both a marketing and brand awareness point of view.

Study what others are publishing so you can be inspired

You don't have to blatantly copy the blogs of other companies or other professionals, but you must always try to be original with respect to them.

Analyze the results of your blog to keep improving

After writing the contents of your corporate blog, you need to understand if they have achieved the desired results.

To analyze the performance of your blog, use tools that are also made available by Google, such as Google Analytics.

You will be able to know how many visits you have received, how users interacted with you and so on. In this way, your company blog will not remain a tool for its own sake, but you will also be able to understand if there are any sections to improve.

To give you an example, there may be articles that do not bring traffic to the blog and therefore will need to be updated or even taken down, as they penalize the overall SEO score of the website. Monitoring the results of your blog is the only way to improve it in the long run.

Chapter 16 - 6 Rules for your Company Blog

We always observe these 6 rules to create a corporate blog that is effective and that reaches the goals it was created for.

Here are the six rules for creating your business blog.

1. If your blog is not on the home page of your site, you should place a button or link in the navigation bar that directs users to the blog. If you don't have a navigation bar, you need to create it.

2. This button must contain the phrase "Blog". You could also call it "Read the blog", or "This is the blog." You do you, try to stand out from the crowd. The important thing is that people easily identify it as a blog.

3. If your blog does not have infinite scroll (like Tumblr for example), that is, if the reader cannot continue scrolling down indefinitely, at the end of each page

you must insert a button that connects the reader to the following pages. "Next Posts" or "Other Posts" are good options for the name of this button.

4. At the end of each post, enter a sharing space or section containing related articles. In short, your reader should not be disoriented once they have read the entire content of the article. This solution is useful for decreasing the bounce rate and keeping viewers on your site.

5. If you offer a particular service, you should give the reader the opportunity to subscribe to that particular service. It could be the RSS feed of your blog, or a newsletter, or even a "Follow me on Twitter or Facebook" option.

6. If in the last 3 months you have used your blog to post links to your podcast or your videos, don't lie to your audience, call this space differently and no longer a blog. And above all, try to correct this and create a useful blog to improve your brand and generate more traffic to the site.

7. Finally, remember to interact with users who read your blog, so as to improve the general User Experience.

Now that we have discussed these simple rules, it is time to dive deeper into the actual strategy to market your company or personal brand through your blog.

Chapter 17 - Winning Strategies for Generating Leads through a Company Blog

We have discussed how a blog is a corporate communication tool that fits within the inbound marketing strategies of a company. Having a corporate blog is not enough, you have to optimize it to reach more customers and potential clients.

This means, you need to create a powerful lead generation strategy that not only gives visibility to your company, but that attracts qualified users to convert into customers.

What are the strategies to implement to generate leads through a company blog?

To generate leads you need to implement 5 winning strategies.

Before talking about these, we want to clarify immediately that Lead Generation is defined as follows.

| *Lead generation is a set of marketing actions aimed at*

acquiring a contact list of site visitors who are really interested in the activities carried out by a company.

It is not merely a question of increasing the traffic and popularity of your blog and business site, but it is about stimulating blog visitors to make a purchase on the web and to increase sales.

Think, for example, of a doctor's office website. In addition to making the blog attractive with content and informative guides that are interesting for the public, the goal is to transform contacts into real customers who make an appointment with the doctor and benefit from the performance and services provided by the clinic.

Through this business model, it is the site visitors themselves who express their interest in the products and services offered and get in touch with the firm, the company or any other professional who has a company website or blog.

You can ask your visitors to just leave their data in an online form to be contacted or to obtain specific communications in exchange or to receive free advice.

Now let's dive deeper into the different strategies.

Strategy 1 - Content Marketing

Writing words is not enough.

The web is full of content, articles, posts, but most of them have little use and little value for users.

A valid Content Marketing strategy begins with planning and developing useful content that has informative power and is of great added value for the audience.

What editorial content do you need to develop?

Posts, articles, guides, infographics, webinars, interviews, research, videos, tutorials are the main tools that act as a lead magnet or a "magnet" able to attract the interest of the public to visit the company blog and conclude a purchase of a company product or service.

A very useful method is to give users the opportunity to read the blog in exchange for some benefits, such as being able to receive exclusive offers and discounts, perhaps even inviting users to subscribe to your newsletter.

Always include calls to action at the end of your posts. Invite your readers to do something at the end of each article, this will increase the engagement and the overall conversion rate of your social media marketing strategy.

Thanks to this little tactic you have the possibility to create a blog to convert leads into real customers.

Strategy 2 - Use Social Media

Interacting and communicating with social media has become increasingly strategic for every company and every professional, don't you agree? We bet you do if you have read this book up to this point.

How important is it, for example, to communicate and make yourself known on Facebook?

On Mark Zuckerberg's popular platform you can select the

market segments to target thanks to the Facebook campaigns service to generate leads. Thanks to this service, you have the ability to "target" posts and content based on the audience you want to reach.

It is an economical and fast strategy that ensures concrete and fast results: the Facebook ad form is very easy and intuitive to fill out.

Strategy 3 - Email Marketing

How important is sending emails to the potential audience you want to reach?

A lot.

Once your business blog has started generating leads, you can use the email addresses obtained to turn them into active customers.

Email marketing is a winning strategy that guarantees a good economic return on investment: recent research has shown that about 66% of consumers have made an online purchase following an email marketing message.

Furthermore, users and visitors of a corporate blog who receive personalized offers and promotions via email spend

127

140% more than those who do not. To turn your mailing list into a powerful lead generation machine, you need to make sure your emails are relevant to your blog's prospect profile.

Strategy 4 - Landing Page

Why are businesses using a landing page more and more? That is a good question.

The answer is simple. They do it to collect the email addresses of visitors to the corporate blog so that they can be transformed into leads. To get a potential customer's email, it is important to offer free resources such as e-books, reports, guides, checklists, etc.

This will encourage them to subscribe to the mailing list: use few fields in the forms, otherwise users may desist from leaving their contacts.

Strategy 5 - Dedicated events

To build loyalty and to generate leads to be transformed into real customers, it is useful for every company to organize events, conferences and live workshops.

In this way, you can constantly attract the attention of the audience and "target" your offer based on the preferences and needs of consumers.

Thanks to these 5 Lead Generation strategies you can save a lot of time to transform the leads and contacts collected into potential customers interested in your products and services. Apply them and you will be closer than ever to success.

Chapter 18 - Creating your Company Blog using Wordpress

WordPress is by far the most used platform for managing corporate blogs. To proceed with the creation and management of a corporate blog, all you have to do is purchase a domain, choose a hosting service and install WordPress.

WordPress is free to download in its basic version. For a more complete service, you can purchase an SSL protocol and guarantee the security of the transfer of sensitive data. With WordPress, you have a number of templates, that is, free or paid themes to give a graphic identity to your corporate blog.

Remember that there is no optimal theme for a corporate blog that is defined in advance. Instead, you should choose a quality and functional WordPress theme, which is representative of your corporate identity.

One thing to keep in mind when creating your corporate blog

is to build it making it as responsive as possible.

Almost 70% of Americans browse the contents on the web from their smartphone.

To be precise, 67% of Americans own a smartphone or tablet that they actively use to surf the web. In 2017 alone, 1.9 billion connections from smartphones and tablets were recorded, already greater than 1.6 connections made from traditional desktop instead.

What does this mean for you?

It means that more than 25% of active web users connect only from smartphones or tablets, favoring new generation portable devices over PCs to do the following things.

- inquire and read content;
- make purchases;
- communicate on social networks;
- network or online promotion for your business.

This means that if your blog is not responsive you are neglecting 1/4 of your potential user base, which is something you do not want to do.

Having a responsive blog is now taken for granted and is considered essential by the average web user. In fact, 22% of users who surf the internet from smartphones leave a website that has obvious problems with navigation or makes viewing of contents extremely slow.

How can I tell if my blog is responsive?

At this point we must therefore ask ourselves an important question. If my blog is the main tool with which we communicate with, promote and finally sell my professionalism, my services and my products, are we sure it is optimized for browsing and reading from smartphones and tablets?

In order to have a positive answer to this question, your blog must follow these standards.

- The texts are not written with a font that is too small and you have to continually "zoom in" to read the contents well by moving along the lines;

- The images are big enough;

-

- The menu is easy to navigate;

- There are no alignment issues between the various parts of the site;

- The social sharing buttons are big enough and you do not have to zoom in to be able to share content.

Then you definitely have a responsive blog.

If you want to carry out an automatic and secure check, you can use online responsiveness verification services, such as Amiresponsive. It is a great tool that tells you whether your corporate blog is suitable for mobile interaction or not. Just enter the correct URL of your blog to check if your blog is responsive or in any case to check for any layout problems.

If your blog is not responsive, we advise you not to delay any longer. Having a responsive blog will allow you to offer your users the best experience. Here are a few steps you can take in order to make your blog more responsive and easier to interact with.

- Make sure people can read your articles comfortably. This is extremely important to create an audience that keeps coming to your blog for more and more content.

- Allow visitors to navigate through tags and categories without problems. Making sure that your blog is easy to search through is such an incredible advantage for your visitors and something you should not forget.

- Access old articles with ease. Some people may come back months after they have read one of your articles. Making sure they are easily able to find it again is a great step towards responsiveness.

- Allow your visitors to share the contents of your most recent article on the various social platforms with a simple click. This simple feature increases the engagement by a lot, so do not sleep on it.

- Allow users to easily fill out contact forms to get in touch with you. An easy communication process between you and your potential clients can be the key to your success.

Having a corporate blog is the best strategy to create value for your company and customers, even if it is by no means an easy feat and there is no ready-made recipe for doing so.

Let's recap the tips to follow to create your successful business blog.

- Establish ad hoc goals so that people become attached to your brand thanks to informative content: Why do we want to start a blog? What do we expect? What do we want to communicate?

- Knowing the potential customers interested in your business is essential because it allows you to establish the type of content to publish.

- Identify content and topics that are engaging, stimulating and consistent for users and in line with your corporate mission with the specific purpose of bringing the right people towards conversion.

- Decide the frequency of publication. Consistency and frequency are essential to be successful when starting a corporate blog.

- Create an editorial plan that helps to organize the work in a meticulous way.

- Carefully take care of the graphic layout of the blog and try to make it as consistent as possible with the visual identity of the brand or company logo.

- Promote the blog to reach the public through social media, guest blogging, pay per click promotion campaigns etc.

- The blog is a "showcase" and a space where customers can constantly interact and leave comments and feedback. Make sure it is easy for them to get in touch with you.

If a customer is not satisfied, you need to be able to handle negative feedback.

You can do this by avoiding censorship and never deleting the negative comment, as it is likely that the user will express his dissatisfaction through other channels promoting an even more negative vision of your company.

Always try to respond politely and always ask the customer the reason for the dissatisfaction. Once you have found out what the problem is, be willing to solve it.

Try to make your dissatisfied customers think again about your company and keep in touch with all the blog visitors as if they were real people. Why? because they are.

Conclusion

Congratulations on making it to the very end of this book, it has been a great journey.

We hope you were able to find valuable information to improve the online presence of your company or personal brand using the power of a responsive blog. We have tried our best to give you every tool and strategy you might need to turn your blog into a money making machine.

Now it is on you to put in practice what you have learned. Because remember that understanding a concept and making it work for you are two totally different things and as an entrepreneur or influencer you should always be willing to take the risk to try and test new strategies.

We are sure that if you commit to seriously working on your business blog, you will be well ahead of competition. After all, it is not a secret that most businesses have a superficial approach when it comes to their online presence, especially when it comes to having a neat and responsive blog. Doing things differently will certainly put you miles ahead of them and will give you an unfair advantage in the long run.

We hope you enjoyed this book and we wish you great success!

CPSIA information can be obtained
at www.ICGtesting.com
Printed in the USA
LVHW032355080221
678731LV00021B/473

9 781801 640565